oxey|l-5·99
19/9/91

# Alexander Graham Bell

by Michael Pollard

**Picture Credits:**
AT&T: 6, 34, 48, 52; Bell Canada Historical Source: 30; The Bostonian Society/The Old State House: 16-7; The Bridgeman Art Library: 12, 13; British Telecommunications: 53, 55 all, 58, 59 below; Mary Evans Picture Library: 8 and 9 (Bruce Castle Museum), 10, 51; Exley Publications: 29 (Nick Birch), 32; Michael Holford: 46; New York Historical Society: 50; Telecom Technology Showcase (British Telecom Museum): 44 top, 47; Telefocus (British Telecom): 4; Library of Congress: 7, 19, 21, 24 and 25 (Gilbert H. Grosvenor Collection), 26, 31 top and 35 (National Geographic Society), 31 below (Gilbert H. Grosvenor Collection), 36, 38-9, 40-1, 45 and 49 and 56 (Gilbert H. Grosvenor Collection), 60 (National Geographic Society); Magnum: 59 top (Eric Hartmann); Royal National Institute for the Deaf: 14-5; Zefa: 54.

Published in Great Britain in 1991
by Exley Publications Ltd,
16 Chalk Hill, Watford,
Herts WD1 4BN, United Kingdom.

Copyright © Exley Publications, 1990
Copyright © Michael Pollard, 1990
**British Library Cataloguing in Publication Data**
  Pollard, Michael, *1931–*
  Alexander Bell
Telephony. Bell, Alexander Graham, *1847-1922*
  I.   Title.
  II.  Series.
  621.385092

**ISBN 1-85015-200-4**

**Series editor: Helen Exley**
Picture research: Caroline Mitchell and Elizabeth Loving
Editorial: Samantha Armstrong and Margaret Montgomery
Typeset by Brush Off Studios, St Albans.
Printed and bound in Hungary.

# Alexander Graham Bell

*The story of the invention of the telephone —
and its effect on our lives*

## Michael Pollard

**≣EXLEY**

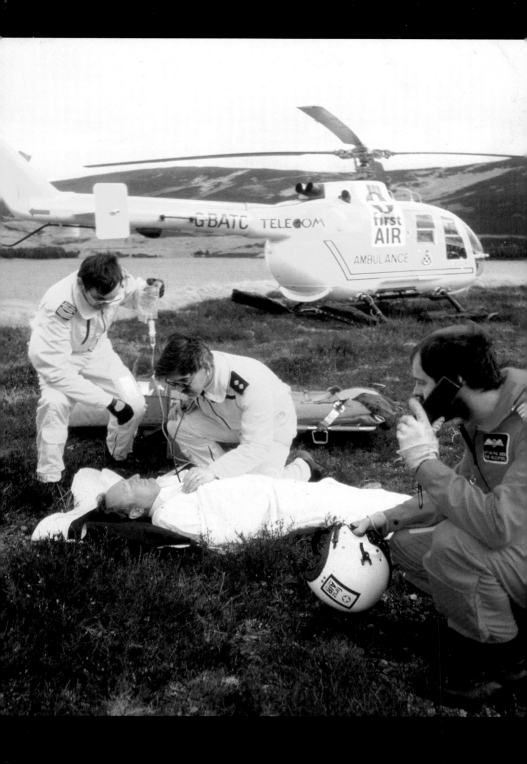

# Suspense

Among the passengers on the morning train from Boston to Washington on Saturday, February 26, 1876 was an anxious and impatient young man aged twenty-eight. He was fashionably but quietly dressed in the business wear of the time: long dark cutaway coat, high waistcoat, and white shirt with a black bow-tie under a wing collar.

He seemed unable to settle. From time to time he got up and paced the length of the coach. Frequently, he took his watch from his waistcoat pocket and glanced at it. He tried to read his newspaper, but couldn't concentrate. Now and again, he took out a notebook and wrote a few words in it.

The young man had good reason to be agitated. If things went well, he was on his way to make a fortune. If they went badly, he was on his way to nowhere. His name was Alexander Graham Bell.

# A dream come true

A telegram had arrived the previous night at Bell's home in Boston. It was from his business partner, Gardiner Greene Hubbard, and it told him to leave for Washington as soon as possible.

Hubbard had gone to Washington two weeks before. There, he had filed details of an apparatus Bell had invented to carry human speech over wires. This apparatus already had a name – the telephone – but as yet there was no working model. So far, Bell had managed to send only vague and indistinct noises over his telephone. But he was confident that he was nearing success. All his life, Alexander Graham Bell had dreamed of making a world-shaking invention. It seemed now that his dream could come true.

*Opposite:*
*Telecommunications affect almost every aspect of our lives, but never more vitally so than in the links they provide for the emergency services. By radiotelephone, these paramedics can report back to base, seek advice, and arrange for the hospital's reception of their patient.*

5

*On the verge of breakthrough: This portrait of Alexander Graham Bell shows him in the attic laboratory in Boston where he and his assistant Tom Watson worked feverishly to perfect the telephone ahead of their rivals.*

It was this that had made Gardiner Greene Hubbard's trip to Washington vital. His aim was to secure a patent for Alexander Graham Bell's telephone. By giving full details of an invention and obtaining a patent, an inventor can prevent anyone else from copying the idea and profiting from it. The idea becomes the inventor's property. It can be sold to anyone else, or a fee can be demanded from anyone who wants to use it in business. In the USA, at that time, a patent lasted for seventeen years. After that, it "ran out" and was free for anyone to use.

## The rivals

But Alexander had not been alone in his research. This was the reason for his hurried trip to Washington. He needed to be on hand in case officials at the United States Patent Office wanted to question him. Another inventor, Elisha Gray, had come up with an almost identical idea, and had applied for a patent on the very same day. It was up to the officials of the Patent Office to decide whether it would be Gray or Bell whose name went down in history as the inventor of the telephone.

The outcome of their patent applications was crucial for both men. The winner would make a fortune from the right to make and sell the telephone all over the United States, and eventually all over the world.

On his arrival in Washington, Alexander Graham Bell faced an anxious wait while Patent Office officials made their decision. "You can hardly understand the state of uncertainty and suspense in which I am now," he wrote to his father. Friends arranged a busy social life for him to take his mind off his worries, but the vital decision was never far from his thoughts.

## Another threat

Then Alexander heard an even more worrying piece of news. It seemed that a *third* application for a telephone patent had arrived. And it was in the name of someone who, although the same age as

Alexander, was already famous as an inventor: Thomas Alva Edison. Edison, Bell learned, had the backing of America's leading telegraph company, the mighty Western Union.

The management of Western Union were ruthless, powerful men with influence in US government circles in Washington. They had made huge profits from the telegraph business and had limitless money to spend. Alexander had financial support from his partner Hubbard and another investor, but it was nothing compared with the money Western Union could spend on supporting Edison. Alexander's character was honest and open, and he hated double-dealing. He was both angry and hurt when he suspected that some of the people he met around Washington while waiting for the result of the patent applications were commercial spies planted by Western Union.

For the past nine months he had toiled almost to the point of exhaustion, combining work on his

*The operations room of the Western Union Telegraph Company. Founded in 1851, the Western Union had, by ruthless business methods and by buying out small local companies, achieved a commanding position in the telegraph industry by 1875. The telephone was a threat to the company – unless it, too, could market a telephone system.*

## Dots and dashes

A number of inventors produced telegraph machines which allowed messages to be sent instantaneously over wires, but it was an American, Samuel Morse, who invented the machine that was finally adopted. It was based on the electromagnet. This is a piece of iron with a coil of wire around it. When electric current flows through the wire, the iron becomes magnetized and, like all magnets, attracts iron. When the current is switched off, the magnet effect stops.

Morse also invented a code of dots and dashes to represent the letters of the alphabet. To send a telegraph message, the operator tapped out the words in Morse code. When the operator pressed the key of the transmitter, an electrical circuit was completed and a burst of current went down the wire to the receiver. This magnetized an electromagnet which attracted an iron pin. When the pin hit the electromagnet, it made a sharp tap. The operator at the receiving end translated the short taps ("dots") and long taps ("dashes") back into

*The main London telegraph office in 1871. The operators are receiving and decoding the Morse messages printed on paper tape, and passing them on to local offices for distribution. The telegraph, and later the telephone, provided more interesting employment opportunities for women at a time when the main alternative was domestic service.*

10

the words of the message, or the taps were marked with a pencil on a moving reel of paper.

Using different arrangements of dots and dashes, Morse code covered all the letters of the alphabet, all the numerals from zero to nine, and even punctuation. The famous Morse code message was the emergency signal SOS – three dots (S) followed by three dashes (O) followed by three dots (S). On a paper tape it would come out like this:

$$\cdots --- \cdots$$

Morse set up the first public telegraph system, covering the thirty-seven miles between New York and Baltimore, in 1844. Soon, telegraph companies were operating between all the main towns and cities of the North American east coast. In the 1860s, after the American Civil War ended, the rail network pushed westward across the United States and telegraph lines ran alongside. Soon, every trading post and station had its telegraph office to send and receive messages.

## Busy lines

The telegraph was a much faster means of communication than anything that had been known before, but it had drawbacks. If you wanted to send a telegram, you had to go to the telegraph office. The message itself, in the "dots" and "dashes" of Morse code, arrived quickly, but at the receiving end it had either to be delivered to or collected by the recipient. If there was a reply, this cumbersome procedure had to be gone through in reverse.

Sending a telegram was also costly compared with a letter. For this reason, private telegrams tended to be restricted to urgent messages, such as news of family deaths, and for many people the telegram never lost its association with bad news.

Although the technology of the telegraph was simple, making use of it as a means of communication was expensive. It needed a network of sending and receiving offices, all linked by lines, staffed around the clock. Landowners demanded fees from companies for permission to run lines over their land, and it was costly to put up the lines.

Nineteenth century
Edinburgh, where
Alexander Graham Bell
was born in 1847, was the
heart of Scottish
fashionable and cultural
life. Alexander grew up in
an intellectual
environment similar to
that he was to find in
Boston, Massachusetts.

Once up, they had to be maintained and repaired. Only the largest companies could afford the expense of setting up an efficient network, and in the United States two companies, Western Union and the Atlantic and Pacific Telegraph Company, dominated the telegraphy business.

However, the telegraph was a great boon to businesses, especially to those with their own telegraph offices. It made it possible to schedule and signal trains safely and to transmit news reports quickly. By 1870, the first submarine cables had been laid under the Atlantic Ocean and there was direct communication by telegraph between North America and Europe.

Both the Western Union and the Atlantic and Pacific Telegraph Company had invested heavily in setting up their networks, and were looking forward to their rewards in terms of big profits. For business, the telegraph had quickly become a must. This was why the news that more than one inventor was working on a "speaking telegraph", as the telephone was called at first, was so unwelcome to the

telegraph companies. The telephone would be a threat to the telegraph business, and the companies could answer it in one of two ways. They could either use their networks to carry telephone as well as telegraph messages, or they could patent the telephone themselves and then sit on the idea while they continued to make money from telegraphy. Either way, the first inventor to patent the telephone stood to make a great deal of money. This explains the keen interest of the telegraph companies in what Alexander Graham Bell was doing, the Western Union's hiring of Edison to invent a rival machine, and the involvement of investors like Bell's backer, Gardiner Greene Hubbard. He saw the chance of making a fortune.

*Emigrants facing a long, uncomfortable and hazardous voyage, are seen off at the quayside by their families. For many, the parting would be for a lifetime. A lucky few might receive letters from emigrants who had made good inviting their families to join them. But not all were as fortunate as Bell in finding prosperity in their new home country.*

## Migrants from Scotland

Alexander Graham Bell arrived in North America from Scotland in 1870, just as the development of the telegraph was reaching its peak. He was twenty-three.

13

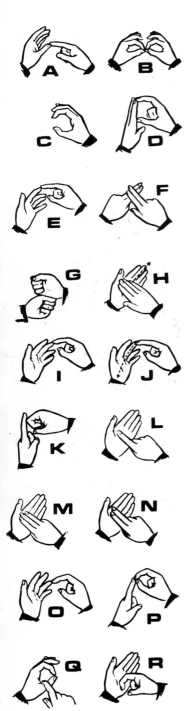

It was an exciting time to be in America. The year before, the Union Pacific and Central Pacific railroads had met in Utah, completing the first trans-continental rail link and opening up the Midwest. The scars of the American Civil War were beginning to heal. American industry was booming. Canada, too, was developing, though less quickly.

Alexander's father and grandfather were teachers of elocution and gave speech therapy, trying to cure such problems as stuttering. His father had developed a system of writing which he called "Visible Speech", based on symbols which showed how the lips and tongue should be arranged to make particular sounds. Alexander's father – also called Alexander – was immersed in his work with Visible Speech. He had a dominating personality, and insisted that his three sons should learn Visible Speech and take part in demonstrations of it. There was some interest in Visible Speech among elocution teachers, but Alexander senior was disappointed when he tried to persuade the British government to recommend it for state schools. In 1868, he had been on a lecture tour of the United States in the hope of finding more interest there.

## Children in a silent world

Alexander senior had become interested in the problems of "deaf mutes" – that is, people who had been born deaf or had gone deaf so young that they had little or no experience of hearing speech. As a result, they had no opportunity to learn to speak by imitation, which is the way that children with normal hearing learn. Alexander senior thought that Visible Speech could help them.

Alexander Graham Bell – "Graham" was an additional name that he chose for himself as a schoolboy – was born on March 3, 1847, the second of three sons. His brother, Melville, was two years older and Edward a year younger. Both brothers died of tuberculosis as young men, within three years of each other. It was this that led the Bell family to move to North America. There, they hoped, the environment would be healthier – for young Alexander had never been very strong. American educators were also more welcoming to Visible Speech.

## The heavy father

But Alexander himself did not want to go. He was teaching at a school for the deaf in London, using Visible Speech among other methods. He had started a degree course at London University. He had found someone he wished to marry, and was only waiting for the opportunity to propose to her. Above all, he wanted to make his own life, out of his father's shadow.

Alexander senior was a typical "heavy father" of the nineteenth century. It would not have occurred to him that his son should not do exactly what he wanted him to, even to the extent of marrying a wife of whom he totally approved. He had expected all three of his sons to follow him into the family "business" of speech training. He had denied them independence by refusing them money unless they asked for and accounted for every penny. He was to continue to shower Alexander with unwanted (and usually unheeded) advice until well into Alexander's thirties, and to make Alexander feel guilty about his wish to go his own way.

## To Canada

But, as their only surviving son, Alexander felt it was his duty to go with them, although this would lessen his chances of breaking free of his father's influence. In those days, families divided by emigration rarely met again. After a long night spent walking the streets, trying to make up his mind, Alexander decided that he could not say goodbye to his parents for ever. He abandoned his studies, wrote a final sad letter to his girlfriend and, on July 21, 1870, sailed with his parents for Quebec.

He watched the English coast recede with a heavy heart. At twenty-three, what had he achieved? He was still treated like a child in his father's household. He had been virtually forced

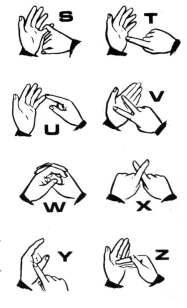

*Opposite and above: The two-handed alphabet used today to communicate in sign language with deaf people has been developed from earlier versions of "Sign". It is still the subject of fierce debate between those who believe it to be the best means of communication for the deaf and those who argue that it excludes them from normal life.*

*Boston, when Alexander arrived in 1871, was a place of commerce with a thriving seaport – seen here – and was busy with cultural and scientific activity. Eager to learn and make a name for himself, Alexander had no difficulty in adjusting himself to the life of the city and taking advantage of the opportunities it offered.*

into a career as a teacher of the deaf, and depended on his father's contacts for work. He had turned his back on further qualifications, and on the marriage and independence that he longed for. And all for an uncertain future.

Alexander was not to know that, for him as for millions of other people from Europe, North America was to prove a land of opportunity.

## Beginning again

Alexander Bell senior was right in his hunch that America might be more interested than Britain in Visible Speech. Inspired by one of his 1868 lectures, a teacher named Sarah Fuller had started a new school for the deaf in Boston, and on hearing that he was in America again she got in touch with him.

The result was that in the spring of 1871, the young Alexander left the new home the Bell family had set up at Brantford in Canada, moved to Boston in the USA, and began teaching at Sarah Fuller's Boston School for Deaf Mutes.

It was an ideal solution to Alexander's personal problems. He would be doing work of which his father approved, and indeed the only work in which he had any experience, and he would be away from home and able to develop his own ideas and interests without interference.

## Boston

Boston was, and still is, one of the USA's most cultured cities. Its public library was the largest in America. In 1866 the world-famous Massachusetts

Institute of Technology, the M.I.T., had been founded there. The city was at the heart of art, music and cultural activities of all kinds. It was an ideal base for a young man like Alexander with wide interests and an insatiable curiosity. He threw himself enthusiastically into his new life. Handsome, witty, and a very good pianist, he was a welcome newcomer to Boston dinner parties.

Now independent of his father, Alexander was able to make his own decisions and take charge of his own life. He developed experimental ways of teaching deaf children and, in the evenings, deaf adults. He was now committed to a career as a teacher of the deaf. Although he still used his father's Visible Speech system with some pupils and occasionally demonstrated it to other teachers, he was developing his own methods.

"My feelings and sympathies are every day more and more aroused," he wrote to his parents. "It makes my heart ache to see the difficulties the little children have to contend with."

## The patient teacher

He discovered for himself something that was almost revolutionary in those days: that children responded better to sympathy and patience than to the bullying methods that were more usual in schools then. He worked hard to get his deaf pupils to understand and experience, if only at second hand, the world of sound.

He would explain how vibrations made sound waves which, in turn, produced vibrations in the ears of people with normal hearing. He would get the children to hold a balloon while he spoke with his lips against it so that they could feel the vibrations. He would demonstrate with a feather how the breath was controlled in speaking. He would place the children's hands on his larynx so that they could feel the vibrations of his vocal cords as he made different sounds. In this way, they learned to distinguish between pairs of sounds which are very similar, such as "p" and "b" or "s" and "z". He convinced children who had never heard a sound in their lives that they, too, could learn to speak and make themselves understood.

His success with children whose parents had feared would never speak was remarkable, and his fame as a teacher of the deaf quickly spread far beyond Boston.

## The Hubbard family

At this point in his life, Alexander met the wealthy lawyer and businessman who was to back him over the next few years.

Gardiner Greene Hubbard had made a fortune from the growing rail network and water and gas supplies. He was a successful lawyer, a Massachusetts senator, and a typical business leader of the North American boom years. Only one thing clouded his life. Of his three children, only one, Mabel, survived infancy, and when she was five she became totally deaf as a result of scarlet fever. The

*Alexander Graham Bell stands at the top right of this group photograph taken at the Boston School for the Deaf in June 1871, soon after he joined the staff. Sarah Fuller, who had invited him to the school, is second from the left in the next row down.*

19

only words she could speak were the few she had learned as a toddler, and even these had become grotesquely distorted.

Hubbard used his considerable wealth and influence to obtain the best education possible for Mabel. He was determined that she should learn to speak normally. He hired a governess for her, sent her to a special school in Germany, even opened a school near his home for her. Mabel was very intelligent, she excelled at her schoolwork and she became an expert lip-reader. However, her speech remained very poor.

In 1873, Alexander Graham Bell was appointed professor of speech and elocution at Boston University's School of Oratory. This was a tremendous compliment to his success at Sarah Fuller's school, and to the impression he had made with his lectures on the science of speech. Among the people who came to see him at the university was Mabel Hubbard, now fifteen. Alexander agreed to take her on as a pupil and to try to improve her speech.

Alexander's teaching achieved their aim in a way she and her parents did not expect.

## Sign versus speech

Both Bell's appointment to the School of Oratory and Hubbard's choice of him as Mabel's teacher were a tribute to the particular method of teaching deaf people that he had developed.

There were – and still are – two basic methods. One is to use Sign language, spelling out words and ideas with the fingers in a kind of code. There are many versions of Sign, but the version most often used was developed in France in the eighteenth century from the language that deaf people in Paris had worked out for themselves. Sign enables deaf people to communicate with each other and with others who have learned it. However, critics argue that it limits them to the world of other deaf people.

This was Bell's view. His father's Visible Speech was an attempt to improve on Sign by teaching deaf people to form vowels and consonants and thus to be able to communicate more freely with people

*"I think I can be of far more use as a teacher of the deaf than I can ever be as an electrician."*

Alexander, writing to Mabel, 1878.

with normal hearing and speech. It was one of a number of techniques for teaching deaf children to speak using what is known as the "oral method".

The argument between those who preferred Sign and those who preferred the oral method divided teachers of the deaf. The oral-method teachers argued that deaf children should be taught to live as near normally as possible in the world of speaking and hearing people, and that if they were of normal intelligence they could be taught to speak. Sign, these oral teachers said, condemned deaf children to live as second-class citizens in a prison of silence. Not so, argued the teachers who preferred Sign. Sign enabled those who had learned it to communicate better and more deeply because the sheer grind of learning by the oral method limited the pupils' vocabulary and ability to express ideas.

There was another angle to the argument. Many deaf children had been taught to speak, but their speech sounded so different that they seemed

*Mabel Gardiner Hubbard aged about six. A year earlier, she had contracted scarlet fever. This is now an easily-treated disease, but in the nineteenth century it could be extremely dangerous and could lead to lifelong complications. One of these was that inflammation could spread from the skin to the inner ear, resulting in incurable deafness which was what happened to Mabel.*

21

to be mentally handicapped. In the nineteenth century, many people felt that it was better for a child to be "mute" than to be thought "mentally defective".

Alexander Graham Bell's methods brought about a change by showing children *how* sounds were made and by improving the quality of the speech of his pupils. But the "Sign or sound" argument is still going on, and many therapists who believe in Sign still blame Alexander Graham Bell for having popularized the "oral method".

## The spare-time scientist

Busy as he was, Bell still enjoyed the hobby of scientific experiments. He found that telegraphy was both exciting and accessible. It needed little equipment, and this was easily obtainable or could be made at home. As an amateur it put Bell in touch with some of the most interesting new technology of the time, and as telegraph equipment was still in its infancy there was always the possibility – or at least the dream – of accidentally stumbling across a profitable and famous breakthrough. In the early days of radio, many enthusiasts were attracted to it as a hobby for similar reasons.

Bell had always been interested in the telegraph. When he was still in his teens, he and a friend had rigged up a wire between their houses over which they exchanged messages in code. He had also experimented with combining what he knew of telegraphy with the understanding of sound that he had gained from his father.

He had become interested in how the human mouth could make so many different sounds, and in particular how the vowels were formed. Experimenting with a tuning-fork held in front of his mouth, he found that the movement of his tongue, as he formed it for different vowel sounds, altered the pitch of the fork – in other words, vowel sounds were related to musical pitch.

This discovery had already been made by a German scientist, Hermann Helmholtz, who had made an apparatus to sound tuning-forks to required pitches by means of electricity. A friend translated Helmholtz's account of his work for Bell, and although he did not fully understand it, he grasped the basic idea – that electricity could be used to generate sounds of different pitches and values. This was an advance on the telegraph, which offered only sound or no sound, according to whether the current was flowing from the sender or not. There was a long way to go between Helmholtz's apparatus and the telephone, but already, by the time he was nineteen, Bell had taken the first step. His first thought was that the power of electricity to generate different pitches of sound might be used to help deaf people.

In fact, Bell was getting closer to an understanding of the relationship between electricity and sound which underpins the modern recording and radio industries. In addition to his work on the telephone, he was to play a part in the beginnings of sound recording and was only prevented from developments in many other fields by the lack, during his lifetime, of the basic technology. He would have been delighted to know that today people with severe speech difficulties are able to speak with the help of synthesizers, microcomputers which use electricity to generate sound.

*"When people can order everything they want from the store without leaving home and chat comfortably with each other by telegraph over some piece of gossip, every person will desire to put money in our pockets by having telephones."*
Alexander, in a letter to Mabel, November 1876.

## Telegraph delays

One problem with the early telegraph was that only one message at a time could be sent over a line. When demand was high, this caused delays and defeated the telegraph's aim of rapid and instant communication. Busy telegraph offices were often full of people waiting to send or receive messages. For example, someone behind a news reporter with a long article to send was in for a very long wait.

The problem was infuriating for the telegraph companies, which saw that if they could increase the capacity of their lines they would be able to do more business. There was a rich reward waiting for the inventor who could come up with a successful idea. And it was into this race that, almost by accident, Alexander Graham Bell stumbled.

## The harmonic telegraph

By 1872, telegraph companies were installing an improvement – the duplex system. This allowed one message to be sent in each direction at the same time, but it could not help if, for example, there was a whole batch of messages waiting to be sent in one direction. Thinking about this, Alexander Graham Bell remembered Helmholtz's experiments and his own, and had the idea of a "harmonic telegraph". If electricity could generate different pitches of sound, could not a mixture of pitches, each carrying a different message, be sent over a wire at the same time and "unscrambled" at the receiving end?

It was still in Alexander's mind that the electrical production of different pitches could in some way help his deaf pupils, but he became more and more interested in applying the idea to the telegraph. In the winter of 1872-73 the twenty-five-year-old Bell began to work seriously on the harmonic telegraph project, experimenting through the night and largely in secret. He was very wary (rightly, as it turned out later) about discussing his ideas with anyone else in case they were stolen. He read as much electrical theory as he could, but he had no practical experience with electricity and, working by trial and error, he had little success.

This was the stage he had reached when, in 1873, he had been offered the professorship at Boston University, and for a while he had had to put his experiments aside.

*Replicas of the "harmonic telegraph" instruments which Alexander Graham Bell and Thomas Watson used for their historic breakthrough in June 1875. The vibrating reed at the top of each instrument was the key to Alexander's invention. The reed in the receiver responded to vibrations set up in the transmitter reed.*

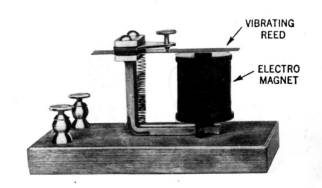

VIBRATING
REED

ELECTRO
MAGNET

By the next winter, he had managed to make a harmonic telegraph which sent simultaneous signals on two different pitches. He continued experimenting, but another matter was increasingly on his mind. As it turned out, it was less of a diversion than it might have seemed at the time.

## Alexander in love

Alexander was falling in love with one of his pupils, sixteen-year-old Mabel Hubbard. But, for nearly two years, he kept this to himself. He was ten years older than Mabel, and a prosperous business owner and politician might not be very keen for his daughter to marry a comparatively poor university professor. This would not be the "good marriage" for which Mabel and her parents had hoped, and even if Mabel accepted Alexander's proposal, it seemed unlikely that her father and mother would.

Alexander's reasons for keeping quiet would have been stronger still if he had known that, even after he had been teaching her for two years, Mabel could write that "I never never could love him or even like him thoroughly." However, he spent as much time as he could with the friendly and lively Hubbard family, which was so different from the earnest, rather serious Bell household back in Ontario. At the Hubbards', he discovered something about Mabel's father, Gardiner Greene Hubbard. Hubbard, it turned out, was also interested in telegraphy and in ways of increasing the capacity of telegraph lines – for business purposes.

*"I know I am not much of a woman yet, but I feel very very much what this is to have as it were my whole future life in my hands.... Of course it cannot be, however clever and smart Mr Bell may be; and however much honoured I should be by being his wife I never never could love him or even like him thoroughly.... If Mr Bell does ask me, I shall not feel as if he did it through love. You need not write about my accepting or declining this offer if it should be made. I would do anything rather than that."*

Mabel Hubbard, in a letter to her mother, July 1875.

## Hubbard's plan

Hubbard had some reservations about the Western Union Telegraph Company. He accused Western Union of holding back progress in telegraphy so that it could continue to demand high prices for telegrams. The answer, he said, was to set up a rival service making use of the new technology and using post offices as stations where telegrams were sent and received. Hubbard reckoned that this would halve the cost of sending telegrams and make them almost as cheap as letters.

This was his argument. The truth was that Hubbard had spent most of his business life building up service industries like water and gas supplies, and telegraphy was another such industry whose profits he wanted to share. The only way of breaking the power of the two telegraph giants was to find a more economical way of operating a telegraph system. When Bell told him about his experiments with the harmonic telegraph, Hubbard saw that it was the key to setting up a rival telegraph service.

*Alexander Graham Bell (right) and Thomas Watson in the Exeter Place laboratory in Boston which was financed by Gardiner Greene Hubbard and his partner Thomas Sanders. This picture was painted in March 1877, when Alexander was struggling with the problems of turning the telephone from a novelty into a serious means of communication.*

A crisis was now approaching in Alexander Graham Bell's life. He enjoyed his work at the university and his private teaching, especially when Mabel Hubbard was his pupil. But he was becoming more and more interested in his work on the harmonic telegraph. His sense of urgency was increased when he heard that Elisha Gray was also working on similar lines.

Gray had limitless time in which to pursue his experiments. Bell had to fit his in with a busy academic and professional life. If he had known that Edison was also at work in the same field, funded by the Western Union, Bell's anxiety would have been even greater.

As it was, Alexander's position was worrying enough. With little time to spare from his teaching, and with no money to buy equipment or to rent a workshop, he was up against a rival with both.

At this point, Gardiner Greene Hubbard made Bell an offer. Hubbard would fund Bell's experiments in return for a share of the profit – if Bell managed to register his patent first. He would also organize the patent application. The father of another of Alexander's pupils, Thomas Sanders, also agreed to put up some money. It looked as if Alexander Graham Bell's show was on the road at last – provided he could overtake Elisha Gray.

## A neck and neck race

By November 1874, Bell was in no doubt of the score. "It is a neck and neck race between Mr. Gray and myself who shall complete our apparatus first," he wrote. Assessing his chances, he thought that Gray had an advantage with his knowledge of electricity, but that he, Bell, knew more about the science of sound.

Hubbard's and Sanders' backing enabled Bell to hire a part-time assistant and rent a workshop in Boston. The assistant was twenty-year-old Thomas Watson. The decision to employ him was one that Bell took reluctantly. He was, by nature, someone who preferred to work on his own, and he was also worried about his secrets leaking out.

*"If I succeed in securing that Patent without interference from the others, the whole thing is mine and I am sure of fame, fortune and success if I can only persevere in perfecting my apparatus."*
  *Bell, in a letter to his father,*
  *February 1876.*

But Watson was the perfect choice. He was as enthusiastic as Bell, as prepared to work long hours, and as determined not to even think about the possibility of failure. There was no doubt that he was completely loyal and trustworthy. Best of all, he was a skilled electrician who made up for the gaps in Alexander's own knowledge.

By the spring of 1875, Bell and Watson had developed the harmonic telegraph to the point where it was ready to be registered at the Patent Office. It was still not reliable, and endless tinkering, adjustment and improvement would be needed before any telegraph company would be interested in it, but they were both satisfied that the principle was right.

## Breakthrough

An ordinary telegraph receiver responded to any burst of electrical current sent along the wire. The principle of Alexander's harmonic telegraph was that the transmitter and receiver had a number of steel reeds, each tuned to a different pitch in pairs. Messages could be sent between each pair of reeds at the same time, but a reed in the receiver would respond only when the transmitter reed with the same pitch was used to transmit current. The pitches chosen for the reeds had to be far enough apart to avoid the possibility of a receiver reed responding to more than one transmitter reed. Provided this was done, a single wire could, in theory, carry as many messages as there were pairs of tuned reeds.

On June 2, 1875 Bell and Watson were working on the apparatus when one of the three sets of transmitters and receivers developed a fault. It did not transmit its pitched note.

The transmitters and receivers were in different rooms, linked by a single wire. Alexander Bell was in the transmitter room, and he went through to ask Thomas Watson to switch off the current, see whether the reed of the faulty receiver had jammed, and if so to free it.

By the time Watson had found the faulty reed, Bell was back with the transmitters. When Thomas

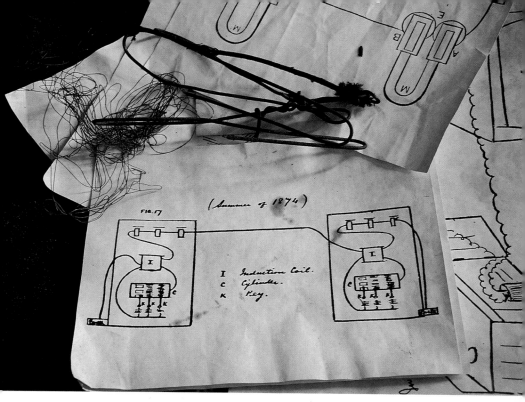

Watson flicked the sticking reed free, the reed of Bell's transmitter vibrated enough to give an audible sound. The vibration caused by Watson's finger prising the jammed reed free had been transmitted to Bell's apparatus in the other room.

Was it a breakthrough, or a mere accident?

Bell and Watson changed places and tried again. Again they had the same result. The meaning of this was clear: sound itself could be transmitted in electrical form, and translated back into sound at the other end. But what was even more remarkable was that this had happened when the electrical current was switched *off*. Bell and Watson reasoned that a small amount of magnetism had been left in the electromagnet when it was switched off, and it was this that had made the reeds vibrate and sound. The fault in the apparatus that afternoon had turned the dream of the "speaking telegraph" or telephone into reality. There was a long way to go, but that day the telephone was born.

*Unlike his competitors, Alexander had no lavish equipment or team of assistants to help him develop and refine his ideas. His only companion in his laboratory was Thomas Watson, and they made their own apparatus using odds and ends from a friendly supplier of telegraph parts. Alexander's laboratory notebooks were filled with hastily sketched diagrams like those shown here.*

*Opposite top: Gardiner Greene Hubbard, Alexander's patron, partner and father-in-law. It is unlikely that, without his friendship, Alexander (opposite below) would have been anything more than a part-time, hopeful inventor. It was Mabel Hubbard (below) who brought the two together – at first as a pupil of Alexander's and then as his wife.*

## Backing two horses

Bell, already overworked and with other claims on his time, now had two projects to cope with – the harmonic telegraph and the telephone. His backer Hubbard wanted him to concentrate on the first. This seemed more likely to have commercial possibilities, whereas the telephone seemed little more than a clever toy – and one that needed a lot more work done on it.

Hubbard was right, but he had reckoned without Bell's enthusiasm and determination. He also reckoned without the streak of stubbornness in Alexander's character.

Alexander's love for Mabel Hubbard was known by now in the Hubbard household, and Mabel had revised her opinion of him a little. She did not love him yet, she told him, but she no longer disliked him. Despite the half-hearted sound of this, Alexander started to court Mabel seriously. He was encouraged by Mabel's mother, who had always had a soft spot for him ever since he had started visiting the Hubbard home.

Now, Mabel's father hinted to Alexander that only the profits from the harmonic telegraph would provide enough money for Alexander to marry her. To Bell, this sounded like blackmail, and he reacted angrily. For a few days, the future of the partnership hung in the balance. If they had parted company it is likely that Elisha Gray would have gone down in history as the inventor of the telephone. However, both Hubbard and Bell backed off, and Bell continued as before to work on both projects.

## Engaged

Another result of this domestic crisis was that on Mabel's eighteenth birthday, Thanksgiving Day 1875, she and Alexander became engaged. When the public holiday was over, Alexander returned immediately to his work.

Bell had succeeded in sending a sound of a particular frequency over a wire, but he knew that there was a big gap between this and sending speech. The sound of a human voice is made up of a whole range of sound waves. These waves vibrate at different rates called frequencies. Different people's voices use different parts of this range. This is why children's and women's voices are higher than men's. But even within the range of frequencies that we can use as men, women, boys or girls, our own individual voices use only some of the frequencies. For this reason, we can recognize one person's voice from another's, even if we are too far away to hear the words distinctly.

If the telephone was going to be able to carry a human voice, Alexander realized, it must be able to transmit and receive a wide range of frequencies. It was not necessary to transmit every one of the frequencies. Even modern telephones don't do this. They cut off the top and bottom frequencies. This is why the voice of someone you are listening to on the telephone does not sound exactly the same as if he or she were in the same room, and why sometimes you cannot recognize the voice of someone you know quite well on the telephone.

## Changing frequencies

How could a large number of different frequencies be turned into changes in an electrical current, and how could the current be changed back again into sound frequencies at the receiving end? To find the answer, Bell's thoughts turned to what he had learned, as a teacher of the deaf, about how the voice and the ear work.

The sound of speech is produced by vibrations of the vocal cords in our throats. The sound waves travel through the air to the listener's ear. They produce identical vibrations in a part of the ear called the ear-drum. This is a thin, tightly-stretched piece of skin called a membrane. The vibrations of the membrane are picked up by the nerves in the ear and transmitted to the brain.

Was there, Bell wondered, a way that he could copy the vibrations of the vocal cords and ear-drum so that the wide range of frequencies produced by the human voice could be sent along a wire as electrical signals?

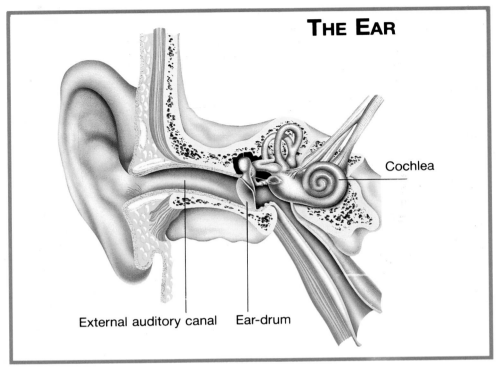

# THE EAR

Cochlea

External auditory canal    Ear-drum

*Alexander took as his model for the telephone the workings of the human ear, which he knew from his studies in speech therapy. Sounds enter the ear as vibrations which strike the membrane of the ear-drum and set up vibrations in response. The vibrations then pass along three small bones to the cochlea, the snailshell-like organ to the top right. In the cochlea, the vibrations are turned into nerve signals which are sent on to the brain. Alexander's idea was that in the telephone the membrane, or diaphragm, would receive the sound vibrations which would then be changed into electrical signals.*

## Imitating the ear-drum

He decided that there was. The answer was to imitate the membrane of the ear with a device called a diaphragm. This was a sheet of material thin enough to be vibrated by the sound of the voice, and also thin enough to vibrate in response to small changes in electrical current. Attached to the middle was a magnetized reed, which moved when the diaphragm moved. The reed moved inside an electromagnet, and as it did so the sound vibrations were turned into changes in current. These changes in current went along the wire to the receiver. There, they made the receiver's diaphragm vibrate, changing the signals back into the original sound.

On July 1, 1875, Bell tried out his new diaphragm telephone for the first time by singing into it. Watson, listening on the receiver in the next room, heard him – not clearly enough to be able to distinguish the tune, but it was a step forward.

For a time, Bell's work on the harmonic telegraph

and the telephone went on side by side, with Hubbard still urging him to spend more time on the telegraph and Bell and Watson snatching as many moments as they could to develop the telephone. A new year, 1876, dawned. For Alexander Graham Bell, it was the make-or-break year. He and Watson, both dangerously close to nervous exhaustion from overwork, somehow found a last-minute burst of energy in the first weeks of the new year. They drew up the telephone patent application which Hubbard took to Washington in mid-February.

## Down to the real work

Returning to Boston with the patent for the telephone, Alexander was, of course, overjoyed. But he knew that the granting of the patent was just the first step. It was only a description of how he proposed to set about making a telephone. To patent an invention, the inventor did not have to supply an example of the apparatus. Alexander had yet to actually make a working telephone. Also, somewhere ahead in the future, was the question of whether the telephone would work over longer distances than the passage between the two rooms in Exeter Place where Alexander had set up his laboratory.

Alexander wasted no time. By March 8, the day after he returned from Washington, he and Thomas Watson were hard at it in the laboratory, which was above a restaurant. The set-up was ideal for a hard-working inventor with no time to waste. Bell slept in one room and worked in the other. For his snatched meals, he went downstairs to the restaurant.

Two days later, Watson was listening on his receiver in Bell's bedroom while Bell spoke into the transmitter. Bell wrote a detailed account of what happened next in his laboratory notebook.

Bell shouted into the mouthpiece of the transmitter the words "Mr. Watson, come here. I want to see you." Watson rushed through and said that he had heard and understood the message. Bell

*"I am afraid to go to sleep lest I should find it all a dream, so I shall lie awake and think of you."*
Alexander, in a letter to Mabel after their engagement, November 1875.

*"I rush from one thing to another and before I know it the day has gone! University – Visible Speech – Telegraphy – Mabel – visiting – etc. etc. – usurp every moment of my time, and I cannot manage all that I lay myself out to do.... There is a great deal of hard work before me."*
Bell, in a letter to his parents, February 1876.

*Above: March 9, 1876: Alexander's moment of triumph. Tom Watson (right) rushed into the laboratory to report excitedly that he had heard Alexander calling him. Opposite: In the 1870s, photography was still fairly new, and studio portraits like this one of Alexander were taken by professional photographers. This shows a serious-minded, thoughtful young man with perhaps a suggestion about the mouth and chin of stubbornness – or determination.*

asked him to repeat it, and he did so. Then they changed places and Bell listened while Watson read from a book. The results were not quite so good. "The effect was loud but indistinct and muffled," wrote Bell, "but an occasional word here and there was quite distinct. Finally the sentence 'Mr. Bell, do you understand what I say?' came quite clear and intelligibly."

## Busy days

Fizzing with excitement, Bell and Watson took turns in sending messages to each other. "How do you do?", they asked each other. Bell sang a verse of the British national anthem. Hubbard was invited to Exeter Place to hear the telephone in use. A few days later, Bell's father called to experience the miracle. Day after day, Bell and Watson tried out

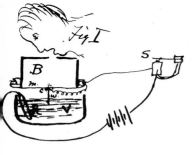

Alexander's sketch of his first successful harmonic telegraph, from the entry in his laboratory notebook on March 9, 1876. His notes read: "A membrane (m) was stretched across the bottom of the box (B). A piece of cork (c) was attached to the centre of the membrane (m) forming a support for the wire (w) which projected into the water in the glass vessel (V). The brass ribbon R was immersed in the water also. Upon singing into the box B, the pitch of the voice was clearly audible from S, which later was placed in another room."

"I often feel as if I shall go mad with the feverish anxiety of my unsettled life. I do so long to have a home of my own, with you to share it."
Alexander, in a letter to Mabel, April 1877.

new ideas, new variations, new improvements. The results became more and more reliable.

It was enormously exciting for Bell and Watson to be in at the beginning of this new technology. Every new step was a great leap forward. But anyone used to today's telephones would have thought Bell's apparatus a poor thing. The speaker had to shout into the mouthpiece, and the listener would – with luck – hear a faint, distorted sound at the other end, often accompanied by cracklings and rustlings. The struggle to turn this primitive instrument into a world-wide means of communication was to be a long one, in which other people as well as Alexander Graham Bell would play a part.

But all this excitement was only one side of Alexander's life. He was still a full-time professor at Boston University, and had lectures, class lists and exam papers to think about. He was also now, since their engagement, writing daily to his fiancée, Mabel Hubbard.

## Late nights

How did he manage to pack so much into his day? The answer was that Alexander had got into the habit of working through the night, free from interruption, until about 4 a.m. and then sleeping until mid-morning. These erratic hours, combined with rushed meals in the restaurant below his rooms, dashing to his lecture hall and back again to the laboratory, all took their toll on his health, which had never been strong.

However, there was a new task in which Bell had to take part. This was to interest the public, and particularly the investing public, in the telephone. Outside the handful of scientists and inventors who had been involved with it, the telephone was virtually unknown – and to any ordinary person who heard about it, it sounded like an impossible miracle. Who could believe that a device had been invented that enabled you to talk and listen to someone miles away? The task of getting people to take the telephone seriously was not helped by the fact that some of the claims made for the telephone in the newspapers were highly exaggerated. Journalists' imaginations were running far ahead of what Bell and Watson had actually achieved.

There were other questions. Who was to put up the money for lines, for the telephones themselves, and for exchanges? Was the telephone really going to be an addition to the quality of life, or was it, as Hubbard had believed, only an interesting toy? When the *New York Times*, in an editorial, foresaw the possibility of opera, speeches in Congress, and sermons from churches being fed by wire into people's homes, it all sounded very intriguing, but it was hardly enough to get the public wildly excited. These attractions did not mean much to most people.

## Fear of the telephone

Then there were the worries, encouraged by some newspapers (and perhaps by Western Union, which wanted to hold on to its telegraph business). Would having the telephone be like letting a spy into your house? Would everyone else on the line be able to hear what you were saying? If electricity could carry voices down the line, could it also carry disease? Could the telephone actually hurt you? Could it make people go deaf or even mad? What would God think about it? There was no shortage of people who found verses in the Bible which seemed to forbid the use of the telephone, two thousand years before it was invented.

No scientist or business leader took these worries seriously, but it was important that they should be overcome if a nationwide telephone system were to be built up. So Alexander added to his work a publicity campaign designed to make the telephone publicly acceptable. He knew that it was important for him to get his name in the papers and get himself and his ideas – now that he had registered his patent – talked about. He was an impressive and experienced public speaker, and, like many good teachers, had a touch of showmanship in his personality.

One of his first "stunts", designed to get people talking, was performed at a meeting in May 1876 of the American Academy of Arts and Sciences.

*"The telephone is mixed up in a most curious way in my thoughts with you. Even in its present condition I think the instrument can be made a commercial success – so I give you fair warning that it won't be long before I claim a certain promise – oh! I forgot! It was I that made the promise and not you! However I shall claim it all the same!"*
Alexander, writing to Mabel, November 1876.

*The Centennial Exhibition grounds in Philadelphia, 1876, with the exhibition halls in the background. The Exhibition was staged to celebrate one hundred years of the United States' independence from Britain and to show what the "new country" had achieved commercially and technologically in that time. It was an ideal showplace for Bell, who was truly in the forefront of scientific achievement.*

At the meeting, Alexander pressed a key on his lectern, and the audience was amazed to hear, from a box on the table, a hymn-tune.

In a building along the street, Mabel's cousin, William, was playing a "telegraphic organ". Its keys were linked by telegraph line to the box in the lecture hall. The organ transmitted each note, on its particular frequency, to tuned reeds in the box, and these responded to the signals.

The staid academic audience went wild with admiration – and Bell duly got his name into the papers. But, in fact, what he had demonstrated was not the telephone but an ingenious application of the principle of his harmonic telegraph.

## A surprise for the Emperor

An opportunity for publicity came with the Centennial Exhibition in Philadelphia in 1876. Large exhibitions of trade and industry were very popular in the second half of the nineteenth century. They enabled manufacturers to show off their latest wares, and visitors to see what new goods were available. In particular, they were showplaces for new inventions, and the exhibition organizers awarded medals for the most promising exhibits.

For America, the Centennial Exhibition was particularly important. It was intended to celebrate the achievements of the United States since they became independent from Britain, the USA's recovery from its Civil War, and the fact that the United States was rapidly catching up with Britain, France and Germany as one of the world's leading industrial powers. The exhibition at Philadelphia would be getting world-wide attention, and it was an opportunity not to be missed by Bell.

What happened at the Centennial Exhibition became, in Bell's old age, one of his most repeated stories. The exhibition was closed to the public on Sundays, but on June 25 it was specially opened to allow a party of distinguished visitors to go round the exhibits in peace. The party included a number of American scientists, together with Emperor Pedro II of Brazil and a leading Scottish scientist, Sir William Thomson (later Lord Kelvin).

According to Alexander's memory of that day, the visitors proceeded slowly around the hall and spent a good deal of time at a stand where Elisha Gray was exhibiting. The visitors were tired and were about to call it a day when they were persuaded to see Bell's demonstration.

*"Among all these inventions, there was one which not only contributed most to the fame of the [Centennial] Exhibition, but established the name of the United States as a nation of brilliant inventors. Yet it was merely a simple device which its inventor, Alexander Graham Bell, publicly presented there for the first time under the name of 'telephone'.... When it became known that the telephone could speak, almost as perfectly as the human mouth, rendering the spoken words audibly even at a considerable distance, its fame spread like wildfire."*

From the Dutch scientific journal, "De Natuur", 1876.

## "I hear, I hear"

Alexander's exhibit included his harmonic telegraph and also a telephone receiver. Wires ran to the transmitters about one hundred yards away. He had arranged a semicircle of chairs on which the visitors were invited to sit. After explaining and demonstrating the harmonic telegraph, Alexander turned to the telephone receiver. Then, leaving William Hubbard in charge of the exhibit, he went to the transmitter. Sir William Thomson was invited to put the receiver to his ear. To his amazement, he heard first a snatch of song and then Bell's voice asking him, "Do you understand what I say?"

The next to try the new marvel was the Emperor of Brazil. For him, Bell recited the famous "To be or not to be" speech from Shakespeare's play, *Hamlet*. The Emperor jumped up, astounded. "I hear, I hear!" he cried.

Then, as now, newspapers were eager to report the doings of royalty, and the Emperor's astonishment was the big story in the next day's Philadelphia papers. But what pleased Bell most was the reaction

*"Five minutes' conversation is about as much as thirty pages of letter paper, and infinitely more intelligible. All the boasted civilization of the nineteenth century has not been able to give us anything even remotely suggesting an equivalent for a chat over a quiet pipe."*

Unidentified Scottish scientist, 1871.

*Distinguished visitors gather round Alexander Graham Bell's exhibit at Philadelphia. His appearance at the Centennial Exhibition was important in two ways. First, it attracted publicity. The Exhibition received pages of newspaper and magazine coverage. Second, it was an opportunity to introduce Alexander's invention to visiting scientists and industrialists whose encouragement and support was vital to make the telephone a sound business proposition.*

41

of his fellow-Scot and fellow-scientist Sir William Thomson. Sir William asked if he could come back later with his wife for another demonstration. The result was that Sir William was to become the ambassador for Bell's telephone in Britain.

## Long distance

The real test of the telephone's usefulness, however, was its ability to carry voices over long distances, using telegraph lines. Bell now set out to extend its range by slow steps. He and Watson exchanged conversations at two miles' distance, five miles, sixteen miles.

Although he was not business-minded by nature, Alexander Bell was aware of the commercial rewards to be made if the telephone became a serious and practical means of communication, and he was impatient to achieve that goal. There were two reasons for this. First, he wanted to make enough money to marry Mabel. Second, as he wrote to her, "I want to get enough to take off the hardships of life and leave me free to follow out the ideas that interest me most." Many of these ideas were still concerned with the teaching of the deaf, to which he was still giving a great deal of his time.

## News by telephone

North Americans really woke up to the possibilities of the telephone in February 1877, when Bell, almost thirty years old, demonstrated it in front of an audience at Salem, Massachusetts. Fourteen miles away, in Boston, was Watson. They exchanged songs, conversation, and the first news report to be sent by telephone. This appeared in the Boston *Globe* the next day with the headline: "SENT BY TELEPHONE. The First Newspaper Despatch Sent by a Human Voice Over the Wires." The story was copied by other newspapers all over North America, and was reported in scientific journals in Europe.

Not everyone was enthusiastic. The defeated Elisha Gray dismissed Alexander's telephone. "It only creates interest in scientific circles," he wrote,

*"It is indeed difficult, hearing the sounds out of the mysterious box, to wholly resist the notion that the powers of darkness are somehow in league with it."*
From a leading article in the "Providence Press", 1877.

*"As I placed my mouth to the instrument it seemed as if an electric thrill went through the audience, and that they recognized for the first time what was meant by the telephone."*
Bell, describing the Salem demonstration, 1877.

"and, as a scientific toy, it is beautiful, but we can already do more with a wire in a given time than by talking." The telephone, he believed, would never supersede the telegraph. Neither had he been impressed by the demonstration at the Philadelphia Exhibition. All he had heard, he said, was "a very faint, ghostly, ringing sort of a sound."

The telephone also excited the suspicions of the superstitious. It must be remembered that to hear a disembodied voice was then a complete novelty; sound recording had not yet been invented. The only disembodied voices most people had heard about were in ghost stories. To some, the voices coming from the telephone were uncanny, supernatural, even evil. One American newspaper even suggested that the telephone was an instrument of the devil. It was not the first or last time that a new invention came up against the opposition of closed minds.

*A modern artistic treatment of Bell's and Watson's experiments with the harmonic telegraph. It captures the spirit of what many people felt when they read about the experiments in the 1870s. Was Bell a "mad scientist" who was challenging the accepted laws of nature? Was Thomas Watson somehow under his spell?*

ERIC FRASER

GRAHAM BELL'S TELEPHONE 1876

PRD 149

*Right: One of Bell's experimental models, dated February 1877, designed to make the telephone more convenient to use. This was known as the "double pole" telephone, which could be used to listen as well as to speak.*

*Opposite: The telephone provided an opportunity for cartoonists to poke fun, and at the same time to touch on deep-seated fears. But it was not until the coming of radio fifty years later that worldwide rantings by demented orators became a reality.*

*Below: Another variation, demonstrated in late 1877, used separate listening and speaking instruments. It was vital to devise an instrument that could be used with the dignity that nineteenth century conventions required.*

## Improvements

Another problem that had to be solved was the design of a "user-friendly" telephone instrument. The models that Bell had demonstrated involved bellowing into a box standing on a table and then bending the ear to the box to hear the answer. Bell designed improved models, but it was a design by another inventor, William Channing, that became the first instrument in general use. It was a one-piece instrument that was used alternately as a mouthpiece and an earpiece. This slowed up telephone conversations considerably and led to a great deal of confusion.

On April 4, 1877 an electrician for whom Watson had worked, Charles Williams, became the first person to be "on the telephone" on a permanent basis. A line connected his Boston shop with his home. Soon, more people wanted to have the new invention in their homes, and this raised a commercial question: should customers rent their telephones or buy them outright? The decision was eventually for renting, though this meant that less money came immediately to Bell and his partners.

But to get the telephone system off the ground Bell and his associates needed a network of lines. Negotiations with Western Union came to nothing. The giant of the telegraph industry was still anxious not to damage its telegraphy business or to hold up telegrams by sharing its lines with the telephone.

# THE DAILY GRAPHIC

## AN ILLUSTRATED EVENING NEWSPAPER

### 39 & 41 PARK PLACE

| VOL. XIII. | All the News, Four Editions Daily. | NEW YORK, THURSDAY, MARCH 15, 1877. | $12 Per Year in Advance. Single Copies, Five Cents. | NO. 1246. |

TERRORS OF THE TELEPHONE—THE ORATOR OF THE FUTURE.

In any case, as it turned out, the heavy telegraph lines were not suitable for the telephone. In July 1877, Alexander Bell, with Gardiner Greene Hubbard, Thomas Saunders, who had given Bell early financial backing, and Thomas Watson, formed the Bell Telephone Company.

Another contract affecting Alexander's life was signed the same month. On July 11, Alexander Graham Bell married Mabel Gardiner Hubbard. They sailed to Europe for an extended honeymoon which included a demonstration of the telephone – by royal command – to Queen Victoria.

## The greatest enemy

By this time, the summer of 1878, the newspapers and scientific journals were printing excited reports about the possibilities of the telephone. The French magazine *La Nature* had an account, with a picture, of a public telephone booth being used by the police to summon help for a man hurt in a traffic accident. Almost certainly, at that date, this was either completely imaginary or a publicity stunt. Many of the news stories about the telephone owed more to imagination than to fact, but this did not worry Bell, Hubbard and Watson. Indeed, Bell was responsible for some of the fanciful ideas that appeared in the papers. Any publicity was good publicity.

Although there was no shortage of press coverage about the telephone now, there was little enthusiasm among the public. People were less keen to sample the new communications miracle than its inventor had expected. By June 1878, only a hundred telephones had been sold. By August there were six hundred, and by the end of the year 2,600. But no one could say that the telephone was taking North America by storm.

It was a similar story in the other countries where Bell had patented the telephone. His company had met its greatest enemy – public apathy. What was happening was, in fact, what often happens when something new comes on to the market. People are naturally cautious. It took several years for television to "catch on" enough to threaten its great rival, the cinema. More recently, compact discs

were a flop when they first appeared. This reluctance to try something new is due partly to waiting to see if the price will come down, and partly to waiting for further improvements.

## The first telephone exchange

In the case of the telephone, there was good reason to wait for improvements. The first telephone lines ran between one place and another. An owner (or "subscriber", as someone who had a telephone was called, since rent was paid for the line) could speak only to the one other owner to whom the line was connected. There was no exchange system to connect a subscriber with a variety of others, though this was not long in coming.

The first exchange was opened in New Haven, Connecticut, in January 1878. But reception was still poor and there were frequent complete breakdowns. The lines suffered from interference from nearby telegraph lines, and it was often necessary to shout a sentence three or four times before it was understood at the other end.

Many of these early problems were to do with organizing the telephone system rather than with the invention itself, and they were not Bell's concern. He admitted that he had little business flair. "Financial dealings," he once wrote, "are distasteful to me and not at all in my line." So he was happy to leave that side of the Bell Telephone business to Hubbard and to concentrate, at least for a while, on demonstrations and lectures. But even that, too, soon began to pall.

## "Sick of the telephone"

There were three reasons. First, business did not appeal to Bell and he had no talent for it, and once the telephone had been invented, getting it into widespread use was a business matter. Second, in 1878 he became the target of attacks on his claim to have invented the telephone. These came from various directions, but the most damaging were those from the Western Union and Elisha Gray.

*One of the first telephone directories, taking up only one side of a sheet of paper, and with no need as yet to arrange names in alphabetical order! The New Haven District Telephone Company, Connecticut, was one of hundreds of local companies set up in the early days. It was inevitable that these local companies should be combined in larger networks if the telephone was to become a national means of communication.*

LIST OF SUBSCRIBERS.

### New Haven District Telephone Company.

*OFFICE 219 CHAPEL STREET.*

**February 21, 1878.**

| Residences. | Stores, Factories, &c. |
|---|---|
| Rev. JOHN E. TODD. | O. A. DORMAN. |
| J. B. CARRINGTON. | STONE & CHIDSEY. |
| H. B. BIGELOW. | NEW HAVEN FLOUR CO. State St. |
| C. W. SCRANTON. | "    "    " Cong. ave. |
| GEORGE W. COY. | "    "    " Grand St. |
| G. L. FERRIS. | "    "    " Fair Haven. |
| H. P. FROST. | ENGLISH & MERSICK. |
| M. F. TYLER. | New Haven FOLDING CHAIR CO. |
| H. BROMLEY. | H. HOOKER & CO. |
| GEO. E. THOMPSON. | W. A. ENSIGN & SON. |
| WALTER LEWIS. | H. B. BIGELOW & CO. |
|  | C. COWLES & CO. |
| *Physicians.* | C. S. MERSICK & CO. |
| Dr. E. L. R. THOMPSON. | SPENCER & MATTHEWS. |
| Dr. A. E. WINCHELL. | PAUL ROESSLER. |
| Dr. C. S. THOMSON, Fair Haven. | E. S. WHEELER & CO. |
|  | ROLLING MILL CO. |
| *Dentists.* | APOTHECARIES HALL. |
| Dr. E. S. GAYLORD. | E. A. GESSNER. |
| Dr. R. F. BURWELL. | AMERICAN TEA CO. |
|  |  |
| *Miscellaneous.* | *Meat & Fish Markets.* |
| REGISTER PUBLISHING CO | W. H. HITCHINGS, City Market. |
| POLICE OFFICE. | GEO. E. LUM, "    " |
| POST OFFICE. | A. FOOTE & CO. |
| MERCANTILE CLUB. | STRONG, HART & CO. |
| QUINNIPIAC CLUB. |  |
| F. V. McDONALD, Yale News. | *Hack and Boarding Stable.* |
| SMEDLEY BROS. & CO. | CRITTENDEN & CARTER |
| M. F. TYLER, Law Chambers. | BARKER & RANSOM. |

Office open from 6 A. M. to 2 A. M.
After March 1st, this Office will be open all night.

Bell was accused of having stolen Gray's ideas, and of dishonesty in his dealings with the Patent Office. People who had laughed at the telephone as a harmless but useless toy now, seeing its commercial possibilities, wanted to claim it as their own invention. These accusations, and court cases arising out of them, were to go on for nearly twenty years. Bell eventually came to shrug them off, but the first charges hurt him deeply, especially as some of them alleged that he had been made use of, perhaps even made a fool of, by his partner and now father-in-law, Gardiner Greene Hubbard.

Alexander Graham Bell had achieved fame, he had married the woman he loved, his first child – a girl – had been born – and then, suddenly, gossip and malice were taking the pleasure of all this away from him. No wonder that he wrote to Mabel "I am sick of the telephone and have done with it altogether."

## New horizons

But the truth, and the third reason for his withdrawal, was that he was not merely sick of the telephone, but bored with it. He had made the great breakthrough. Let other people refine his idea, make improvements, set up systems and sell the desire for a telephone to people all over the world. Let them argue, if they liked, about who actually invented the telephone, so long as he had his income from the patent rights and his share in the Bell Telephone Company. Bell had a restless, inquiring mind. It was this that had led him to the invention of the telephone in the first place. His income now left him free to do what he wanted. He wasn't sure what, except that he was no longer interested in the telephone.

And there was something else. Since he was a boy, Bell had dreamed of becoming a famous scientist. Now he was one, at the age of only thirty-one. What was he going to do with the rest of his life? If he had known then that he would live for another forty-four years the question may have been even more pressing. Many people would have been

> "The more fame a man gets for an invention, the more does he become a target for the world to shoot at."
> Bell, writing to a friend, 1878.

Boston was the birthplace of the telephone, and it was right that it should also be the site of the first telephone exchange, opened in 1877. This photograph is a reminder of the large number of jobs created by the telephone for line erectors, maintenance engineers, and – hidden inside the building – operators to connect calls.

happy to tour the world as a lecturer, receiving applause, meeting famous people. But Bell was not made like that. "I must," he told his wife, "be accomplishing something."

## The doctor's mad wife

Meanwhile, after a slow start, the telephone was taking off. In 1880, Bell was on a train in North Carolina when it broke down. The train conductor approached him, touching his cap.

"Excuse me, sir," said the conductor, "are you the inventor of the telephone?"

"Yes," said Alexander.

"Do you happen to have a telephone with you?" asked the conductor. "We need to talk to the nearest station and ask for help."

Bell had to explain that, even if he had a telephone in his pocket, the conductor's idea simply wasn't possible. It was an illustration of how the public had not completely understood the principle.

*Opposite: Masses of telephone wires along and across the streets did nothing for the appearance of city skylines, especially as many cities – like New York, here – were proud of their architecture.*

*Below: The main telephone exchange in Paris in 1904. Exchanges were staffed mainly by women for whom the invention had provided clean, respectable and reasonably well-paid work. The early telephones tended to carry higher frequencies best, and so women's voices sounded clearer.*

There was another story about a woman who went to her doctor. "The doctor's wife has gone mad," she reported to her husband later. "She had a box on the wall, and kept talking into it, pretending she was speaking to someone."

The telephone reached Montreal, in Canada, at about the same time as an epidemic of smallpox. The disease was being spread, it was said, down the telephone lines. It took a troop of soldiers to disperse the mob that gathered outside the telephone exchange.

## Edison's improvement

But, steadily, improvements to the system were being made. Perhaps the most important of these was made by Bell's old rival, Thomas Edison. Bell's diaphragm instrument acted very well as a receiver, and an improved version is still used in almost all of the world's telephones today. But as a transmitter, it was less efficient. It had to be shouted at to pick up any sound at all, and the changes in current that it made were too feeble to be transmitted over long distances.

Edison worked on a transmitter in which the magnet was replaced by a small piece of carbon. He had discovered that if carbon was put under pressure – such as the pressure of sound waves – the flow of electricity through it was changed. The telephone transmitter, or mouthpiece, that he developed using this idea was basically the same as the one used today. The principle was also used in the first microphones.

The changes in current produced by the carbon mouthpiece carried over the wires better than those in Bell's diaphragm transmitter, but they needed to be boosted still further – amplified – for long distance calls. This led to Edison's second important contribution to the telephone: the induction coil. This was like a double electromagnet. Wires from the telephone mouthpiece led to an iron bar and were coiled around it. A second coil of wire, with more turns, was also wound around the bar, and then led to the telephone lines. In passing from the first coil to the second, the changes in electrical current were greatly amplified and could be carried over long distances.

## The telephone dial

Other inventors, as time went on, added further improvements to the telephone system. One of the most important of these inventors was not a scientist or an electrician, but Almon B. Strowger, an undertaker, who owned a small-town funeral business.

In the first telephone exchanges, callers were connected by hand to the lines of the people they wanted to speak to. Callers turned a handle to alert the exchange operator, who then asked them which number they wanted. The operator then rang the number, and when there was an answer plugged the caller's line into the line of the other number. This took a little time, and there was also the problem that a nosy operator might listen in to your conversation.

Almon B. Strowger found the system more worrying than most other people. His worry was that when people needing an undertaker rang the exchange, they might be put through to one of his rivals. So he worked on a system that would enable people to dial numbers for themselves. The Strowger automatic exchange, which he invented in 1889, enabled people to do just that. Each number on the dial admitted the caller to the next set of numbers, until eventually the telephone with a particular number rang. Strowger's idea became the standard automatic system all over the world. It is still in use today, though it has been steadily replaced since the 1960s by electronic systems.

Slowly, telephone networks spread. A resident of Boston could, by 1884, talk to someone in New York. Chicago went on the telephone for long-distance calls in 1892, and Bell made the first call from New York. Yet it was not until 1915 that the east and west coasts of the United States were linked by telephone. The progress of the telephone in Europe matched that in America, though at a slower pace.

*Opposite: In the first systems, each telephone was individually connected to the exchange by a separate wire, so huge structures like these (on West Street, New York) had to be built. Apart from being unsightly, they were vulnerable to the weather and to traffic accidents.*
*Below: Underground cables containing large numbers of lines replaced the old overhead system. Here, electricity cables are laid alongside telephone cables to the right.*

It is impossible to imagine any kind of business today that could function without telecommunications, and many businesses depend entirely upon it. These dealers on the Bourse, the Stock Exchange in Paris, receive information about company share prices worldwide from the video screens and buy and sell shares by telephone.

## Music by phone

The dream of the *New York Times* writer, soon after the telephone was invented, that it might be used to bring public events into the home became a reality in the 1880s. The radio broadcasting of music was then still about forty years into the future. A number of telephone companies in America and Europe began transmitting concerts and even plays over their telephone lines. The theatrophone, as it was called, was briefly fashionable, although, according to one report, "the sound produced by the telephones is generally so faint that it becomes

necessary to oblige each listener to cover both ears with telephones during the performance."

Many of the improvements that enabled the telephone to develop were the work of Bell's one-time rival Edison, but Bell was happy to leave Edison to it. He was only concerned that his claim to have been the original inventor was upheld, and this was a battle he would continue to fight until, and even after, the death of Elisha Gray in 1901.

As far as the business side of telephones was concerned, Bell bowed out in 1879, aged thirty-two, leaving the board of directors of the Bell Telephone Company. At about the same time, Thomas Watson also left. He, too, felt that there were other things he wanted to do with his life. For people like Bell and Watson, the excitement of the telephone was over. Other people might get excitement out of building up the telephone business, but not them. Watson treated himself to a tour of Europe, married and settled down as a farmer for a while, and then went into shipbuilding with great success. Bell, happily married, comfortably rich, moved to a new house in Washington and wondered what to do with the rest of his life.

*Top left: The telephone brings communication to a village in the heart of Africa. There are very few places in the world without access to a telephone!*
*Top right: Telephone conversations are beamed across continents by satellite. Above: Cables are still laid for shorter distances, and cable-laying technology has reached a high level of accuracy.*

## Life in Washington

Mabel enjoyed the high society life of Washington, but Alexander grew restless. He was in many ways a loner, and he did not enjoy idle gossip. Much of Washington life revolved around dinner parties given to get the support of politicians for this or that cause. Perhaps remembering his suspicions of politics when he was an unknown inventor, Bell disliked this kind of activity. He believed that facts and arguments should speak for themselves.

In his new-found fame, Bell did not forget his concern for the deaf. He paid for a school for deaf children in Greenock, Scotland, and in 1883 he opened one in Washington, though it closed after two years because he could not find suitable teachers. But he remained active in the education of deaf people for the rest of his life.

Prizes and medals came to him from all over the world. He was made a member of the French Légion d'honneur. He became President of America's National Geographic Society, which he helped to found, and Regent of the Smithsonian Institution, one of the United States' leading scientific bodies. He was constantly in demand for lectures and articles.

## The restless mind

Still, his mind could not rest. A sentence read by chance in an encyclopaedia would set him off on a new train of thought, a new line of inquiry. He read the scientific journals and the newspapers keenly, keeping up to date with what other inventors were doing and often devising improvements to their ideas. The science fiction stories of the French writer Jules Verne set Bell thinking about space travel and underwater exploration, years ahead of the time when the technology was available that would make these things possible.

Following the example of Edison, who had set up an "inventions laboratory", Bell built one of his own at Baddeck Bay in Nova Scotia, and another in Washington. Bell's reasoning was that he had invented the telephone in a makeshift laboratory

*Alexander Graham Bell never lost interest in teaching the deaf. He kept up with new ideas and developments, and continued to inspire specialist teachers in this field. He is photographed here (on the right, with white hair and beard) late in his life at a conference of teachers of the deaf in Tokyo, Japan.*

above a restaurant, with just one assistant to help him. How much more fruitful it would be if he set up purpose-built laboratories, properly staffed, with adequate funds to buy equipment! He was right: over the next forty years, an astonishing variety of ideas came from these laboratories.

Just as Edison had invented the induction coil to improve the telephone system and to make long-distance calls possible, so Bell was able to improve on one of Edison's inventions. This was the ancestor of today's record-player, the phonograph, which recorded and played back sound on cylinders of tinfoil. Although it was hailed as ingenious, Edison's machine had little commercial value, except as a novelty, mainly because the tinfoil cylinders wore out after a few playings. In 1887, ten years after Edison, Bell developed a machine of his own, which he called the graphophone, using longer-lasting cylinders made of hardened wax. The result was another fierce battle, this time with Edison, over patent rights – but it was Bell's machine, with wax cylinders that could be played over and over again, that laid the foundations of the sound recording industry. Later, Bell experimented with an early form of tape recording, though the advanced gramophone was in fact the creation of another inventor, Emile Berliner, in 1897.

## The light telephone

One of the most promising ideas to come out of Bell's later work was what he called the photophone. Late in his life, he was to describe it as his most important invention. This was a device for transmitting sound in beams of light, but Bell never succeeded in sending messages over a longer distance than six hundred feet. The photophone is now regarded as the first step in the development of today's revolutionary optical communications using laser light and glass strands, two technologies which were not available to Bell. Meanwhile, the Italian scientist Marconi was working on radio signals. He managed to send these several miles while the photophone was working only in feet

*"Wherever you may find the inventor, you may give him wealth or you may take away from him all that he has; and he will go on inventing. He can no more help inventing than he can help thinking or breathing."*
*Alexander Graham Bell, 1891.*

*"Can Imagination picture what the future of this invention is to be!... We may talk by light to any visible distance without any conducting wire. In warfare the electric communications of an army could neither be cut nor tapped.... In general science, discoveries will be made by the Photophone that are undreamed of just now.... The twinkling stars may yet be recognized by characteristic sounds, and storms and sunspots be detected in the sun."*
*Bell, writing to his father about the Photophone, 1880.*

and so it was radio that became dominant in the field of communications during the early years of the twentieth century. Bell continued to believe in the possibilities of the photophone for the rest of his life, but it had been overtaken, for the time being, by 1897.

Bell also became fascinated with flying, and built countless kites. He test-ran hydrofoil speedboats, invented an air conditioning system, and even developed a new breed of sheep. In the last year of his life, he was working on a portable system to take the salt out of sea-water, for use in lifeboats. And only a few months before he died, he took part in underwater exploration off the Bahamas.

But despite the hundreds of patents that were registered in Alexander Graham Bell's name, and the wide range of areas of science and technology in which he took an interest, he made his greatest achievement before he was thirty. From the accidental jamming of his harmonic telegraph, he conceived and brought to fruition the idea of the telephone.

## Looking back

In many ways, the rest of his life was an attempt to recapture the heady excitement of those early days. His brain continued to buzz with ideas, but too often, these failed to turn into practical projects.

This was partly because his ideas sometimes outstripped available technology, as with the photophone. Without doubt, too, Bell's own excitable personality led him to raise his own and other people's expectations too high. He made promises he couldn't deliver. In his letters to Mabel and his parents, his accounts of the early telephone experiments were far more glowing than was justified by reality. Within a few weeks of getting the telephone patent he was talking wildly about callers being able to see as well as hear their friends, something that he in fact never attempted and that only developed commercially more than a century later.

This excitability, combined with the hard-nosed commercial instinct of people like Hubbard, played

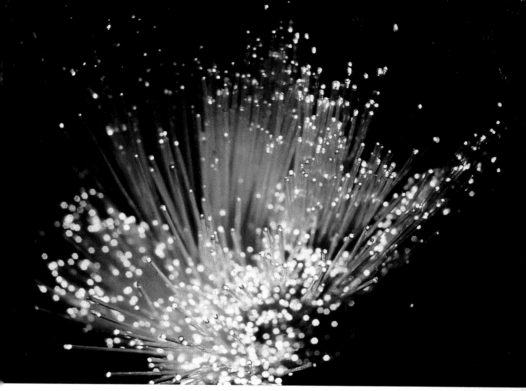

an important part in pushing the development of the telephone from a laboratory experiment to a working communications system. But Bell continued to need the support of the business world more than perhaps he realized. On his own admission, he was no businessman, and the bitter rivalries and law suits surrounding the early days of the telephone sickened him. He longed to "get away from it all".

Baddeck Bay was a refuge where he could combine the pursuit of his own personal scientific interests with a happy family life, emerging from time to time for a lecture tour or foreign travel. Meanwhile, he and his rival Edison lived on into the twentieth century as monuments to the spirit of inventiveness and ingenuity that had helped the United States to achieve technological leadership in many different fields.

Just what an achievement Alexander Graham Bell's breakthrough with the telephone represents can be gauged by comparing the way in which he

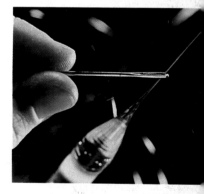

*Above: Telephone development in the future will depend more and more on optical fibres. A single fibre is so fine that it can be threaded through the eye of a needle. Light signals can be passed at a far greater speed than electrical pulses.*

*Alexander Graham Bell's seventy-five years spanned several chapters in the development of science and technology. When he was born, the rail networks had not long been invented. By the time he died, radio broadcasts had begun and the first experiments in television were being made. He always kept up a keen interest in the development of science, but he also gained great pleasure from his family: he is seen here with some of his grandchildren.*

worked, with how inventions so often come about today. When he invented the telephone Bell was a spare-time enthusiast with a senior full-time university job. Even later in his life, when he was prosperous, he was still, at heart, someone who was interested in scientific ideas and followed them up either on his own or with a few trusted helpers.

Today, developments of comparable importance are usually the work of large, well-funded teams of people employed by huge industrial companies or by governments. It is not likely that, in the future, an invention as far-reaching in its significance as the telephone will be the work of someone following an interest in his or her spare time.

## The last tribute

Bell lived long enough to see the start of the next important communications revolution after his own. In the spring of 1922, shortly after his seventy-fifth birthday, he bought a radio and enjoyed listening to some of the first broadcast concerts and sports reports. He was still keeping a notebook of ideas that sprang to his mind, and comments on what was happening at the Baddeck Bay laboratories.

By now, the telephone had spread worldwide; but the United States, with its special need for business and private communication over long distances, was the world's most enthusiastic telephone nation. There were about fourteen million telephones in use, or one for every twelve people – over half of all the telephones in the world.

As usual, Alexander and Mabel Bell went to Baddeck Bay for the summer because they found Washington too hot. Quite suddenly, near the end of July, Bell began to feel weak and lost his appetite. Death came on August 2, 1922 without pain.

The funeral was held two days later at Baddeck Bay. As the service began, the telephone networks of Canada and the United States paid their own last tribute: for one minute, the entire system closed down. It was right that, for a moment, people should be reminded of the man who had started a communications revolution.

# Important Dates

1847   March 3: Alexander Graham Bell is born in Edinburgh, Scotland.

1858   Oct: Alexander enrols at the Royal High School, Edinburgh.

1863   Aug: Aged sixteen, Bell begins teaching at Weston House School "for the Board and Education of Young Gentlemen", Elgin, Scotland.

1866   Sept: Alexander, aged nineteen, takes up a teaching post at Somersetshire College, Bath.

1867   July: Alexander joins his parents in London.
Alexander senior publishes his book on Visible Speech.

1868   May: Alexander joins the staff of a private school for deaf children in London.
Aug: Alexander senior travels to the United States to demonstrate Visible Speech.
Oct: Alexander begins studies at London University.

1870   May 18: Alexander's brother Melville dies, aged twenty-three.
July 21: Alexander and his parents leave for Canada.

1871   Apr 5: Alexander joins the staff of the Boston School for Deaf Mutes.

1872   Apr 8: Alexander meets Gardiner Greene Hubbard for the first time.

1873   Alexander, aged twenty-four, is appointed Professor of Elocution at Boston University.
Mabel Hubbard first receives lessons from Alexander as a private pupil.
Alexander begins his experiments on a harmonic telegraph.

1874   Elisha Gray begins his experiments on a harmonic telegraph.

1875   Jan: With financial support from Gardiner Greene Hubbard and Thomas Saunders, Alexander employs Thomas Watson as his assistant.
Feb: Alexander applies for a harmonic telegraph patent and signs a partnership agreement with Hubbard and Sanders.
June 2: The "sticking reed" in Alexander's apparatus leads to experiments on the telephone.

1876   Feb: Alexander's telephone patent application is presented and is approved on March 3.
March 10: Alexander sends the world's first telephone message.
June 25: Alexander demonstrates his telephone at the Centennial Exhibition in Philadelphia.

1877   Feb 12: Alexander's Salem lecture attracts press attention.
July 9: The Bell Telephone Company is founded.
July 11: Alexander Graham Bell marries Mabel Hubbard.

1878   May 8: Alexander and Mabel's first daughter, Elsie, is born.

1879   Alexander resigns from the Bell Telephone Company and founds a school for the deaf in Greenock, Scotland.

1880   Feb 15: Alexander and Mabel's second daughter, Marian, is born.
Sep: Alexander is awarded the Volta Prize (for scientific achievement in electricity) in France and made an officer of the French Légion d'Honneur. With the prize money, he sets up the Volta Laboratory in Washington.

1881    Aug 15: Alexander and Mabel's son, Edward, is born but doesn't survive.

1883    Alexander opens his own school for the deaf in Washington.
        Nov 17: The Bells' son, Robert, is born but he doesn't survive.

1885    Nov: The Washington school for the deaf closes because of staffing problems.

1886    Alexander buys a summer home at Baddeck Bay, Nova Scotia and builds a laboratory there.

1887    Bell improves Edison's phonograph with his graphophone, the fore-runner of the gramophone.

1890    Alexander helps found the American Association for the Promotion of the Teaching of Speech to the Deaf and becomes its first president.

1898    Alexander becomes President of the National Geographic Society and Regent of the Smithsonian Institution.

1908    Alexander starts his experiments with hydrofoils.

1911    Alexander builds a hydrofoil but it breaks up in trials.

1922    Aug 2: Alexander Graham Bell dies, aged seventy-five.

1923    Jan 3: Mabel Bell dies.

# Further Reading

The official biography of Alexander Graham Bell was not published until 1973, when Robert V. Bruce's *Bell: Alexander Graham Bell and the Conquest of Solitude* (Gollancz, London) appeared. This is a very full and detailed account of Bell's life, and is well worth "dipping into" for readers who are interested in the technical details of his work.

Other books:

Abbott, David (ed.): *The biographical dictionary of scientists: Engineers and Inventors*, Blond Educational, London, 1985.

Jollands, David (ed.): *Language and Communication*, CUP, Cambridge, 1984.

Pollard, Michael: *How Things Work*, Ward Lock, London, 1978.

Seddon, Tony and Bailey, Jill: *Electricity and Magnetism*, OUP, Oxford, 1986.

Whyman, Kathryn: *Hands on Science: Sound Waves to Music*, Franklin Watts, London, 1989.

# Scientific Terms

**Amplify:** To make stronger.

**Audiometer:** An instrument used to test human hearing.

**Carbon:** A naturally occurring chemical element of which coal and soot are made. The carbon used in Edison's first telephone mouthpiece was lampblack – it was used to replace the magnet in the transmitter.

**Diaphragm:** A thin piece of material stretched tightly across an opening. When the material is struck by a *sound wave* it vibrates.

**Dumb:** A word that is condemned by many people because, in addition to meaning *mute*, it can be used to mean "stupid". Deaf people simply have a problem with their hearing. They do not lack intelligence. See *mute*.

**Duplex:** A system which allows messages to be sent in two directions at the same time, over the same wire.

**Electromagnet:** A magnet that is made when a coil of wire is wound round an iron core. The iron becomes magnetized when electricity flows through the wire.

**Frequency:** The number of times a *sound wave* vibrates in one second.

**Hydrofoil:** A type of ship with "wings" or foils which skim the surface of the water.

**Interference:** Noises on a telephone line (or radio) caused by poor connections or other faults.

**Larynx:** The part of the throat that contains the vocal cords.

**Mute:** Literally, silent, unable to speak. In fact, deaf people could learn to speak perfectly, if they could hear. No human being can automatically learn to speak without hearing speech.

**Patent:** The document granting an inventor the right to make, use and sell an invention for a limited period of time.

**Phonograph:** The first machine, invented by Thomas Edison in 1877, for playing back recorded sound. Bell improved it by replacing the tinfoil cylinders with wax ones. This transformed the machine into the successful and popular fore-runner of the gramophone.

**Pitch:** The quality of a sound. It is determined by *frequency*, intensity and loudness.

**Receiver:** A device that receives *electromagnetic* or electrical signals and converts them into an understandable form.

**Sound wave:** A pressure wave that travels through the air at 300m per second. As the wave moves, it creates a disturbance in the air pressure. This disturbance alternates between high and low pressure and is passed from one layer of air to the next. Sound waves can also travel through solids and liquids.

**Telegram:** A message sent by wire and delivered to the recipient by hand.

**Transmitter:** In a telephone, the part that converts *sound waves* into electrical signals that are sent to a *receiver*.

**Tuning-fork:** A metal form which produces a musical note, used for tuning musical instruments.

**Vowels:** The letters *a, e, i, o,* and *u*. Their articulation is made by the absence of any obstruction in the vocal cords. The breath moves through the passage freely.

# Index